CW00719708

Holy Spir

Faith Food Snack Pack

Faith Lifters that Bless and Build Believers

by

Nick Watson

Nick Watson Prophetic Power Ministries

youcanprophesy@gmail.com

www.youcanprophesy.com

My dog Chloe inspired me to write chapter 1. I have also learned much from her mum Libby and brother Jimmy.

Holy Spirit:

Faith Food Snack Pack

ISBN 978-0-9943012-4-6

Published by Nick Watson Prophetic Power Ministries.

Brisbane. Australia. 4178.

ENDORSEMENTS

Pastor Nick Watson broke new ground with his recent book, "You Can Prophesy – Supernatural. Simple. Safe." The book was straight forward, practical and releasing. His latest book is just as impacting and provides insight and wisdom which if applied will bring release to every person who reads it. As I read the book I was encouraged, inspired and motivated to apply the principles it espouses. I highly recommend you read the book and learn from Pastor Nick's personal understanding of profound scriptural principles.

Wayne Swift

National Leader, Apostolic Church Australia;
Senior Pastor, Church 1330. Scoresby. Victoria. Australia.

Firstly I loved it! – great revelation and content with strong Scriptural foundation and support evidenced right throughout the text. The chapters cover a good diversity of subjects with good use of simple illustrations. I like the application questions and Faith Declarations at the end of each chapter. For me as a preacher, it is certainly a great resource for messages, or preaching thoughts.

Gary Swenson

State Ministries Director,

Australian Christian Churches (previously Assemblies of God) Queensland and Northern Territory

Nick's book is full of great material and reads well. I'd describe it as a wonderful discipleship tool. I enjoy working through this sort of material with my staff team – it grows big people. Well done!!

Sheridyn Rogers

Senior Pastor, Network Leader, Activate churches, NZ

Nick Watson's new book lives up to its name! I found it very inspiring. You will find your faith lifted as you read each chapter. It is clear that he is not simply an author, but he has been a faithful pastor for decades. That pastoral grace comes through as Nick shepherds you into a stronger, more vibrant faith that works in every-day life. Enjoy reading Overcoming Faith Food Snack Pack as a solidly biblical and practical encouragement to strengthen your faith in Christ!

R. Sonny Misar

Author, "Journey to Authenticity". Senior Pastor, Living Light Church. Winona. Minnesota. USA

Nick's book is not only easy to read but one which is practical, has depth and encourages genuine discipleship. This book contains a good mix of Holy Ghost revelation, biblical fact and principles. This book poses simple yet effective principles of discipleship that will open our lives to God's favour and His anointing.

Chris Wickland

Senior Pastor, Living Word Church. Fareham. England.

As a minister of the Gospel for over 35 years I have learned to value good, sound teaching. So it is with pleasure that I recommend Nick Watson's new book. Nick is a seasoned prophet and pastor that understands the battles and trials we face daily and I believe his book will prove a blessing in practical teaching on overcoming these adversities of life.

Dr. Col Stringer
Author of 20 Christian books, President International
Convention of Faith Ministers, Australia.

This book is a Biblical gold mine; written to inform truthfully and experientially its readers with life-changing Biblical principles for an exciting, fruitful, loving obedient, Christ-filled "Life!" Throughout the reading of this easy, comfortable, yet exciting writing style of Nick's, he keeps me turning the pages until I become time and again overcome by the wealth of confirmation and witness in my spirit of the treasure truths that are so beneficially needed in our lives at all times.

Rosemary Renninson

International Devotional Writer/Speaker. Moe. Vic. Australia

This is a book I enjoyed and will refer to again and again. For many years I have studied and taught pastoral ministry and done my best to be a good practitioner. This book would have been so helpful! Nick get this published and I will do my best to get it into as many hands I can.

Philip Underwood

Previously National Leader, Apostolic Churches, New Zealand; Senior Pastor (ret.) Cornerstone Church, Philadelphia. PA. USA

FOREWORD

Reading through this book, my heart rejoiced in the wisdom that came through the pages. This is a book of wisdom - and a gift to all believers, but particularly for those called to ministry. And I believe the Holy Spirit has inspired Nick to write this as an inheritance for the next generation of believers.

With many wonderful quotes and anecdotes, Nick imparts to us the blessing of many lessons learned through his years of ministry experience. There are many keys to be discovered by the reader about how to walk in wisdom. Prompting us with revelations and thought provoking stories, Nick has given us a gift that releases hope and help that, if applied, will cause you to walk in greater wisdom and favour.

One chapter had me "Amen-ing" aloud. Take time to absorb and apply the wonderful truths Nick has to share and you will be better for it!

Katherine Ruonala

Author of "Living in the Miraculous: How God's love is Expressed through the Supernatural"

Senior Leader of Glory City Church Brisbane and Apostolic oversight of the the International Glory City Church Network. Founder and Facilator of the Australian Prophetic Council.

www.katherineruonala.com

DEDICATION

My four dedications of this book are:

- To the Lord Who has partnered with me in many ways to write it.

- To my wife Lynne and our family of four generations.

- To the people who have encouraged me in ministry, so that I can pay-it-forward.

- To my great-granddaughter Riley who has inspired all us previous generations by her peace, joy, beauty and hunger for learning and growth

ACKNOWLEDGEMENTS

I thank my amazing wife and the love of my life, Lynne, for being my indispensable partner in life and in ministry.

My thanks also go to all those who have helped me put this book together. Firstly, my chief editor John MacFarlane, without whose skills and efforts this book would not have come into reality. Secondly, my proof-reading family and friends: Pastor Robert Couper, Elizabeth Scrimshaw, Barbara Hodgman, Lynne Watson and Bronwyn Cunningham.

Special mention and gratitude goes to Lisa Watson of the Printing Well, Wynnum for her sensational design of my book covers and other printing help she donated towards this project. *www.theprintingwell.com.au/*

AUTHOR'S CHOICE

I have made two non-traditional choices in this book. Firstly, I have deleted the definite article "the" from the Name of Holy Spirit, because I want Him to become more personal to my readers. Secondly, I have capitalised a lot of pronouns (such as "Him"), in order to give the Lord the honour He is due and to make clear Who the pronoun represents.

BIBLE QUOTATIONS

Contents

INTRODUCTION

This mini-book is one of four taken from my book "Lessons from my Dog: 33 Faith-Lifters to bless and build believers." Each mini-book is a topical collection of life-transforming and equipping messages that cover a variety of subjects.

These are Holy Spirit inspired revelations, Biblical teachings, testimonies and illustrations that have proven fruitful in the lives of many people during my years as Senior Pastor of a thriving Spirit-filled, Apostolic church and travelling prophetic minister.

They will help you develop your God-given potential in Christ and equip you to fulfil your ministry that the Lord has assigned to you, by doing the good works of love and faith that He prepared in advance for you to do. (Ephesians 2:10).

I am honoured by the affirming comments of my anointed, experienced and internationally significant endorsers. Their reviews have confirmed to me that these books are going to meet needs, change lives, multiply ministry, equip believers and fulfil the purposes that the Lord entrusted to me when He anointed me as an author

1 **Lessons from my Dog**
a Wedding Message

How does our little dog manage to wrap two grown people around her little paw? Well, she does. Chloe, our Shih-Tzu, brings great joy into our lives and she also is a great teacher. Here are five life lessons that I learned from Chloe and shared at the wedding of our daughter Rebekah to her now-hubby Pete.

(i)   The first thing dogs are known for is wagging their tails.

This tells us that we only have one life, so we need to make sure it includes having fun and showing appreciation.

In the words of the catchy hit song from the late eighties: "Don't worry, be happy."

Dogs demonstrate their joy so often and so obviously that they could never play professional poker, because whenever they got a good hand, everyone would know they were excited.

There's another thing more people should know about joy. The world thinks God is a killjoy, but the Gospel truth is that He is the Author and Source of joy.

The world thinks God is a killjoy, but the Gospel truth is that He is the Author and Source of joy.

These things I have spoken to you so that My joy may be in you, and that your joy may be made full.

John 15:11 NAS

Rejoice in the Lord always and again I say rejoice.

Philippians 4:4

When dogs wag their tails, they are often communicating something in addition to their joy. They are showing their love and affection for you.

Showing your love for your spouse and being affectionate is an important way to keep your romance alive.

Let your family, friends and colleagues know that you are happy to have them in your life. Affirm people who do a good job. Give thanks to whoever blesses you in some way.

(ii)   The second thing dogs are known for is their loyalty and faithfulness.

I think that lesson speaks for itself. It reminds me of the traditional wedding vow "till death do us part."

Sadly, too many couples these days might as well say "until times get tough, or boring."

Faithfulness is so essential in every area of life. For example, in marriage and family, how many children's hearts have been broken because dad did not keep his promise? How many divorces, with all the heartache it causes for far more than two or three people, have been caused by unfaithfulness?

Another example is that, in the workplace, careers can be made or broken depending on a person's loyalty and trustworthiness.

Remember this: According to the parable of the talents, God expects and rewards faithfulness. He will also, when the time of final judgement comes, punish unfaithfulness. (Matthew 25:14–30).

(iii)   *"He who lies down with dogs, shall rise up with fleas."*

My third doggy-lesson is based on the saying often attributed to Benjamin Franklin. It is about the negative impact wrong relationships can have on our lives.

> *Do not be misled: "Bad company corrupts   good character."*
>
> *1 Corinthians 15:33*

The point is this: be very careful whom you allow to influence your life. In Jeremiah 15:19, the prophet was told to influence others and to not allow people to influence him. That was a mistake that the prophet Isaiah seems to have made, before his transformation and higher calling was birthed when he had a Divine encounter in the temple, in the year that King Uzziah died. (Isaiah 6:5).

Most of us have heard the saying: *"Hurt people hurt people."* The fact is that negativity is catching. Thankfully, so are faith, confidence and joy.

If you want to have a happy marriage, don't bring any fleas home from work or anywhere else.

If you want to have a happy marriage, don't bring any fleas home from work or anywhere else.

Rather, be good for and to each other. Encourage one another to become bigger and better people.

(iv)   "A dog who is chasing his lunch doesn't worry about his fleas."

The fourth lesson is this: Live passionately for the Divine purpose for which you were born. When you do, you won't sweat the small stuff that can be so annoying.

Life is about more than just an endless cycle of: sleep – work – eat – drink – play – sleep – work – eat – drink – play – sleep – work – eat – drink – play – sleep......

Make sure your life includes deeper and more significant things than just the routines of life on earth. Set yourselves some positive goals. Strive to excel and build a worthy legacy to share with and pass on to others. Pursue God's vision and purpose for your (short) life on Earth.

> *[10] And (find out NIV) try to learn [in your experience] what is pleasing to the Lord [let your lives be constant proofs of what is most acceptable to Him]. [15] Look carefully then how you walk! Live purposefully and worthily .., not as the unwise and witless, but as wise (sensible, intelligent people), [16]Making the very most of the time (you have) [buying up each opportunity ... NLT for doing good], because the days are evil. [17] Therefore do not be vague and foolish, nor act thoughtlessly, but understand and firmly grasp what the Lord wants you to do.*
>
> *Ephesians 5:10,15–17 AMP.*

(v)   Don't Make problems for Others; Accept Discipline; Reconcile Quickly

My last lessons can be seen by imagining what happens if and after Chloe disobeys these instructions:

- You shall not bury your bone in the dirt and then bring all that dirt into our nice clean home.

- You shall not chew on my new shoes just because the smell of the leather makes you think they are made of beef jerky.
- You shall not mistake our new green rug for grass and use it like male dogs do a lamp-post or a tree.

My three instructions to Chloe are a useful reminder that we should not create problems for other people to clean up, nor behave in a way that spoils someone else's day.

Here is another thought about what our behaviour should be when someone annoys us. As one doggie commentator wrote: by all means, let others know when they've invaded your territory; but avoid biting when a simple growl will do. In other words, don't over-react to people or things that annoy you.

> *[17]Never pay back evil with more evil. Do things in such a way that everyone can see you are honourable. [18] Do all that you can to live in peace with everyone. [19] Dear friends, never take revenge. Leave that to the righteous anger of God. For the Scriptures say, "I will take revenge; I will pay them back," says the Lord..... [21] Do not be overcome by evil, but overcome evil with good.*
>
> *Romans 12:17–19 NLT and 21 NIV*

When dogs are disciplined, they are put outside. Almost immediately they turn around, wagging their tails because they want to come back in again. This teaches us to never allow offences and resentments to build up in our hearts. Be quick to reconcile when your relationships could be soured by something negative that has happened.

> *In your anger do not sin; do not let the sun go down while you are still angry.*
> *Ephesians 4:26*

The Book of Proverbs has much to say about the importance and benefits of accepting discipline. The Bible talks about the children of God being disciplined by our Heavenly Father, as well as children in family life being disciplined by their parents. There are other authorities who exercise discipline, such as the police and teachers and coaches.

Our attitude toward the discipline we receive determines whether it benefits us or not. Like adversity, it can either make us better or bitter people.

> "My son, do not make light of the Lord's discipline, and do not lose heart when he rebukes you, [6] because the Lord disciplines the one he loves, ...
> [11] *No discipline seems pleasant at the time, but painful. Later on, however, it produces a harvest of*

righteousness and peace for those who have been trained by it.

Hebrews 11:5–6a,11

What is one thing you have learned from this teaching?

_____

What is one thing you can do to implement this teaching?

_____

Faith Declaration:

I thank You Lord for the love and joy I have in my life. I am so grateful for Your faithfulness to me and for helping me build quality relationships with others. I praise You for having a good and significant plan for me to enjoy and to fulfil. By Your grace and my faith I choose to forgive and forget the things that threaten to ruin my relationships and steal my joy. By faith I step into Your good, acceptable and perfect plan for my life, in Jesus' Name. Amen. Help me Lord to accept discipline and counsel in a positive and mature and humble way, so I might benefit from it, as You desire. Anoint me to not cause problems for other people. I declare that I am a good disciple of Jesus and, by the grace given to me and in the power of Holy Spirit, I am a problem-solver, not a problem-maker, to the glory of God.

2

How to Treat
Holy Spirit

But I tell you the truth, it is to your advantage that I go away; for if I do not go away, the Helper will not come to you; but if I go, I will send Him to you.

John 16:7 NAS

What a nonsensical and unwelcome statement of Jesus this must have been to the ears of His disciples. Let's face it, if you had the choice between the visible Lord Jesus Christ, Who went about doing good, healing all those who were sick and oppressed of the devil (Acts 10:38), and a helpful friend of His, Whom would you choose?

However, this is no ordinary friend.

(i)   Who is Holy Spirit?

Holy Spirit is an equal member of the Holy Trinity. (Luke 3:21–22; Matthew 28:19; 2 Corinthians 13:14). Holy Spirit is God because He is Eternal, Omnipotent, Omniscient and Omnipresent. Holy Spirit is a Divine Person, not a thing, such as if He was merely "power" like electricity.

How can you make electricity "grieve"? How can a thing be your teacher, guide or helper. You need a Divine Person to be your source of wisdom, healing, righteousness and strength. There is no vending machine that can enrich your life with all the blessings and resources Holy Spirit is commissioned to impart to you from God.

(ii)   Holy Spirit is for every Christian

> *[38] Peter replied, "Repent and be baptized, every one of you, in the name of Jesus Christ for the forgiveness of your sins. And you wil receive the gift of the Holy Spirit. [39] The promise is for you and your children and for all who are far off — for all whom the Lord our God will call."*

Acts 2:38–39

The wording of this verse tells us that Holy Spirit is for every Christian in every nation and every generation. They may be far off in distance from

Jerusalem or far off in time from the apostle Peter, but when the Lord calls them to come to Christ, then the same Holy Spirit is waiting to indwell and fill them the same as He did on the day of Pentecost and in every generation since.

(iii) Holy Spirit represents Jesus and empowers Christians

Firstly, Holy Spirit indwells the Christian representing the Presence of the Father and the Son. He produces the fruit of Christ-likeness in believers.

Secondly, Holy Spirit fills us and empowers us for supernatural living, in which we reproduce the works that Jesus did.

I want to focus on the empowering of Holy Spirit by considering an Old Testament example, David.

> *So Samuel took the oil and anointed David in the presence of his brothers and from that day on the Spirit of the Lord came powerfully upon David.*
>
> *1 Samuel 16:13*
>
> *One of the servants said to Saul, "One of Jesse's sons from Bethlehem is a talented harp player. Not only that — he is a brave warrior, a man of war, and has good judgment. He is also a fine-looking young man, and the Lord is with him." .....* *[23]And whenever the tormenting spirit from God*

> *troubled Saul, David would play the harp. Then Saul would feel better, and the tormenting spirit would go   away.*

> *1 Samuel 16:18,23*

In verse 23, we learn that Holy Spirit enabled David to get rid of Saul's demons by his praise.

It is important to note here that worship attracts the Presence of God, Who drives out demons. Secular music of any generation has no power to repel demons. Some worldly lyrics today actually attract them.

> *David said to Saul, "Your servant has been keeping his father's sheep. When a lion or a bear came and carried off a sheep from the flock, [35] I went after it, struck it and rescued the sheep from its mouth. When it turned on me, I seized it by its hair, struck it and killed it. [36] Your servant has killed both the lion and the bear; this uncircumcised Philistine will be like one of them, because he has defied the armies of the living God. [37] The LORD who rescued me from the paw of the lion and the paw of the bear will rescue me from the hand of this Philistine." Saul said to David, "Go, and the LORD be with you."*

> *1 Samuel 17:34–37*

David had been overlooked even by his dad, but he was God's choice to be Israel's next king, because of his heart.

David would not have been overlooked if he had already killed the lion and bear. He didn't do those exploits until after Samuel anointed him and Holy Spirit came mightily upon him. Holy Spirit enabled David to slay a lion and a bear and then a giant.

David was a worshipper in the fields with the sheep for years. After the anointing of Holy Spirit, David's worship was empowered to drive away demons.

> *In everything (David) did he had great success, because the Lord was with him.*
>
> *1 Samuel 18:14*

(iv)   How Christians should treat Holy Spirit

(a) Jesus said we must *be "thirsty"* for Holy Spirit and "come and drink".

> *On the last and greatest day of the festival, Jesus stood and said in a loud voice, "Let anyone who is thirsty come to Me and drink. [38] Whoever believes in Me, as Scripture has said, rivers of living water will flow from within them." [39] By this He meant the Spirit, whom those who believed in Him were later to receive. Up to that time the Spirit had not been given, since Jesus had not yet been glorified.*
>
> *John 7:37–39*

We must be thirsty for God (Psalm 42:1,2), not just for an experience. Our thirst must come from our whole heart. (Jeremiah 29:12,13). Then, God is sure to reply. (Luke 11:9–13; James 4:8a).

Let me ask you: "Where are you on the Holy Spirit and Spiritual Gifts continuum?"

- knowledgeable and antagonistic;
- ignorant and antagonistic;
- ignorant and uninterested;
- ignorant but willing to learn;
- knowledgeable and neglectful;
- ignorant and learning;
- open to receiving;
- desiring to receive (i.e. being thirsty);
- committed to receiving, which means desiring and pursuing (i.e. being thirsty and coming to drink);
- learning;
- putting learning into practice by faith;
- zealous with wisdom;
- zealous without wisdom;
- striving;
- faking.

The "thirsting" and "coming" that Jesus talked about means that we must be not merely "open" to receiving Holy Spirit and His empowering, but "committed" to receiving. Holy Spirit is available to anyone and everyone, all the time. Over many years of ministry, I have learned that when a person is spiritually thirsty for this experience, it is a sign that it is not only God's Will for them to receive, but also His Time.

(b) We must *not grieve* Holy Spirit. (Ephesians 4:30).

In the context of this instruction (Ephesians 4:17–5:12) Paul writes to Christians about not grieving the Holy Spirit by doing the works of the flesh. He says I insist that you must not live as the world does. He lists a lot of specific behaviours that do grieve Holy Spirit, including hardness of heart, lust, impurity, bitterness, unwholesome talking and lying.

Paul also writes a number of positive behaviours that attract the empowering of Holy Spirit, such as putting on the new self in Christ, giving to others, forgiving people, showing love and integrity.

Two of the grieving behaviours that I will draw your attention to are, firstly, anger and, secondly, stealing.

> *And "don't sin by letting anger control you." Don't let the sun go down while you are still angry,[27] for anger gives a foothold to the devil.*
>
> *Ephesians 4:26–27 NLT*

Most of our anger is sinful; it is of the flesh. It's your pride or ego that has been offended; or you have been inconvenienced by someone; or you have suffered wrongfully and been hurt or robbed or betrayed by someone. The Bible here says, regardless of the cause of the anger, you should resolve it in your heart before nightfall.

In terms of other Scripture verses about conflict resolution, you should definitely resolve it in your heart and if possible between people before you next take Communion at church. (Matthew 5:23–24).

Righteous anger is when there is an obvious case of injustice. You may have been the victim or perhaps it was someone close to you. The Bible still says you must not stay angry. You can pursue justice without carrying your anger into the battle. Holy Spirit will help you when you seek to obey this instruction. But if you do not aim to subdue your anger, you will grieve Holy Spirit and then He cannot empower you to overcome it and its negative side effects.

Secondly, we see the stunning transformation Holy Spirit can do in someone's life if they do things God's way.

Anyone who has been stealing must steal no longer, but must work, doing something useful

*with their own hands, that they may have
something to share with those in need.*

Ephesians 4:28

What a change of heart this verse represents, as well as a drastic lifestyle change. The thief stops thinking selfishly, as if the world owes him a living. He overcomes whatever internal forces and outward circumstances were pushing him into thievery.

He begins to use his gifts and talents for good, not evil. He wants to make a contribution to the lives of others. He is a living example of God giving more grace, as in 2 Corinthians 9:8.

Another list of things that grieve Holy Spirit is found just before Paul tells us what the fruit of the Spirit is. (Galatians 5:13-25).

To experience the best and long-lasting empowering of Holy Spirit, to build a great life and to leave a lasting legacy, you must build a great character.

Don't be anointed and unholy like secular people who are talented but tainted, such as some famous sportsmen and politicians have been.

To experience the best and long-lasting empowering of Holy Spirit, to build a great life and to leave a lasting legacy, you must build a great character.

If you allow bad things to remain in your life they do not only grieve Holy Spirit, but Ephesians 4:27 says they give the devil the opportunity to attack you. He will turn his opportunity into a foothold and a foothold into a stronghold in your life.

... give the enemy no opportunity for slander"

1 Timothy 5:14b

How much better it is to live so that, if people do talk about you behind your back, it will be good talk.

(c) Do *not resist* Holy Spirit. (Acts 7:51).

Paul, who wrote the advice in Ephesians, learned the hard way to not keep on resisting the Lord. In Acts 26:14, he admitted that Holy Spirit had been prodding him to stop his persecuting behaviour. When Jesus appeared to him, Paul was knocked to the ground and dazzled to such an extent that he didn't see for three days until Ananias prayed for him.

In that Damascus road meeting, Jesus used a word that means ox-goad or cattle-prod. So the promptings of Holy Spirit had not been subtle, but imply that Paul was a strong, stubborn, thick-skinned, stupid bull, who was being hit repeatedly by a long, strong, pointed stick.

The New Testament epistles tell us that our old Adamic, sinful, flesh nature is in opposition to our own regenerated spirit and to Holy Spirit. (Galatians 5:17). Also, our natural man cannot understand the things of the Spirit. (1 Corinthians 2:14). So we must be careful to not slip into a casual spirituality, where we default back to that old nature and find ourselves resisting God.

In Genesis 6:3, the Lord said to an evil world: "My Spirit shall not always strive with man." And that didn't end well for mankind, when the flood came. Only righteous Noah and his family and the animals on the ark survived.

I don't want to frighten you with the reminder of what happened to Ananias and Sapphira when they lied to and put Holy Spirit to the test with their sin. I do not believe that is normal New Testament, New Covenant Christianity.

Neither do I believe that the Lord puts sicknesses on people to get their attention or teach them a lesson. Jesus never did that and He was and is the exact representation of the Father. So, if Jesus didn't do it, then the Father doesn't do it and Holy Spirit doesn't do it.

I do not believe that the Lord puts sicknesses on people to get their attention or teach them a lesson.

However, there are serious warnings in the New Testament concerning "insulting the Spirit of Grace" (Hebrews 10:29) and blaspheming against Holy Spirit (Matthew 12:24–32; Mark 3:22–30), which is saying that something, which is the Spirit's doing, is of the devil.

(d) We are told to *not "quench"* Holy Spirit (Thessalonians 5:19 NIV); nor "stifle" Him (NLT), nor "put out the Spirit's Fire" (ISV).

Sadly, too many Christians do quench Him. For some, it is out of ignorance. They may not have sufficient knowledge about Holy Spirit. Some believers are taught as if the Holy Trinity is Father,

Son and Holy Bible. They are not taught about the Personhood of Holy Spirit.

Three common ways by which Christians quench or stifle Holy Spirit or put out His fire are: by disobedience, when we refuse to obey the Word of God or the leading of Holy Spirit; by un-belief, which is not just doubt but the refusal to believe; by letting fear overcome our faith.

Christians quench and stifle Holy Spirit by their disobedience, unbelief and fear

Let me tell you something the Lord Himself revealed to me. It is so simple, yet so powerful: "Every circumstance of fear is also an opportunity for faith."

(e) The best and right way to treat Holy Spirit is to *fan Him into flame* and stir up your gifts.

(2 Timothy 1:6,7).

When we spend time with God, worshipping, praying and listening, we give Holy Spirit the opportunity to speak and lead us into the God things He wants to partner with us in to fulfil the Will of God on earth.

When we love, give, speak the Word of God, obey and step out in faith in other ways, we activate Holy Spirit, just as God's voice commands did in Genesis chapter 1. Holy Spirit was there hovering, but He didn't spring into action until God spoke.

You have to do something to stir yourself into action, to stir up your faith and to use the talents, resources, spiritual gifts and opportunities God gives you. Then you will know how real, how holy, how wise, how powerful and how empowering Holy Spirit is.

> *For this reason I remind you to fan into flames the spiritual gift God gave you ....*
>
> *2 Timothy 1:6 NLT*

Why don't you give God an extra one hour each week? Use half of that hour to be still before God, worshipping, waiting, reading His Word, listening and asking Him questions like: Lord is there anything You want me to do today?

The other half of that hour is for obedience. Put into action whatever you sense Holy Spirit is leading you to do. If you do not feel you get any specific instructions from Heaven, just do something good, either practical or spiritual, for someone.

As you wait on the Lord in the first half-hour, you become Spirit-filled. This is so that, in the second half-hour, you can be Spirit-spilled into the lives of others. By doing such things you will make God to be real in both your own life and in the lives of the people you touch.

Give Holy Spirit an hour of your life per week more than you are doing now. The first half-hour is for you to receive and be Spirit-filled. The second half-hour is to do something for someone, so that you can be Spirit-spilled in Kingdom ministry

---

My final point is this:

> [17] *Therefore do not be vague and thoughtless and foolish, but understanding and firmly grasping what the will of the Lord is.* [18] *And do not get drunk with wine, for that is debauchery [wild living – ISV; reckless actions – Holman Study Bible]; but ever be filled and stimulated with the [Holy] Spirit.*
>
> *Ephesians 5:17-18 AMP*

The International Standard Version ends verse 18 like this: "keep on being filled with the Spirit."

When I was first saved, lots of years ago, we were taught the following saying; It is founded on New Testament truth, including Ephesians 5:18 and the testimony of Peter in Acts 2:4, Acts 4:8 and Acts 4:31: "One baptism in Holy Spirit, many infillings."

So, please make it a priority to be filled with Holy Spirit and stay filled with Him, because we are needed to be His instruments in this world. Unfortunately, life and ministry can both deplete us. We need to intentionally stay Spirit-filled and to always be thirsty for more of God in our lives, as well as desiring more from God.

What is one thing you have learned from this teaching?

_____

What is one thing you can do to implement this teaching?

_____

Faith Declaration:

I thank You Lord for giving me your Holy Spirit as my Helper. Forgive me Lord for times when I have grieved Him, resisted Him, neglected Him, disobeyed Him or quenched Him. I praise You for the empowering Holy Spirit brings into my life, so that I am more like Christ in my character, behaviour and ministry. I am thirsty for more of You God and more from You Lord, by Your Holy Spirit. Right now I stir up my faith to hear You, to be filled with You and to be used by You. I say here I am Lord, fill me, send me, use me for Your glory and people's benefit, in Jesus' Name. Lord by faith I declare I am ready for both the natural and supernatural things You have in store for me and for others through me. I look not to my feelings, but to You Lord and to Your Word. I declare in Jesus' Name that as I step out in love and faith, Holy Spirit will be activated to do the works God wants done. Amen

3 Holy Spirit, our Standby

From Atmosphere to Action

However, I am telling you nothing but the truth when I say it is profitable (good, expedient, advantageous) for you that I go away. Because if I do not go away, the Comforter (Counsellor, Helper, Advocate, Intercessor, Strengthener, Standby) will not come to you [into close fellowship with you]; but if I go away, I will send Him to you [to be in close fellowship with you].

John 16:7 AMP.

(i) The Advantage of having Holy Spirit in your life

Surely this must have seemed to be the most ridiculous and unwelcome statement Jesus ever made to his closest friends and disciples. It was equalled in its unwelcome-ness by Jesus' predictions of His suffering and death. However, while these passion and triumph prophecies were mysterious, they were definitely not ridiculous.

Put yourself in their place. Would you rather have the visible, personal, wise, miracle-working Jesus with you, or have Him send along someone that you might assume would be like a substitute teacher at school, when your real teacher is away due to sickness?

Another way of putting yourself in their mind-set is to imagine Jesus being like your closest companion, who is a mixture of Bill Gates the richest man in the world, Einstein possibly the smartest man who ever lived and Arnold Schwarzenegger (or whoever was the strongest man in the world).

Whenever you were confronted with an opportunity or a challenge, you could ask Bill to pay for it or Einstein to figure it out or Arnie to break through the obstacle with brute force. That's what it was like for them to have Jesus with them. Can you see how hard it would have been for the disciples to understand how Jesus' departure would be in any way advantageous to them?

What they didn't realise was that they would be scattered to lots of nations and places. Because Jesus was limited to being in a physical body, He could only be in one place at any one time. When the omnipresent, omniscient, omnipotent Holy Spirit came to live inside them, He would be with them and all believers wherever they were anywhere and everywhere in the world, all the time. What an advantage that is.

Jesus gave them, and us, a clue about this Paraclete Who was to come, when He used the clarifying adjective "allos" (in the Greek) to say "another" Helper. (John 14:16 NAS). This Greek word indicates that Jesus was saying the Holy Spirit would be another Helper of the *same kind* as Jesus Himself. In other words, Holy Spirit is a Divine Helper, Whom Christians know to be the third Person of the Trinity.

If Jesus had used the clarifying Greek word "heteros", He would have been telling them that the new helper was going to be a different kind of helper than Himself.

When we understand that Holy Spirit is just as much God as Jesus was, then His prediction makes sense. Jesus could only be in one place at a time, because He had confined Himself to a human body. Therefore, if He was in Jerusalem and He sent the disciples to Galilee, He could not be with them.

On the other hand, because Holy Spirit is as omni-present as God, He can be with each and every disciple in equal measure all the time, even if they are scattered throughout every nation on the face of the earth.

Now that is a great advantage for every believer to have in life and ministry, just as Jesus said – isn't it?

--------~~~~~/\ ~~~~~~~--------

New Testament Christians have the advantage of the Divine, Omniscient, Omnipotent, Omnipresent Holy Spirit with each and every one of us, all the time, everywhere. This is better than having Bill Gates, Einstein and Arnold Schwarzenegger as our companions.

--------~~~~~/\ ~~~~~~~--------

(ii) 7 Holy Spirit descriptions in John 16:7 AMP

I love the seven words the Amplified Bible uses to describe Holy Spirit. Of course, He is many other things as well, including our teacher, our guide, the One Who convicts us of sin, righteousness and judgement to come and sanctifies us, and Who empowers us to grow the fruit of the Spirit and to minister to others using His supernatural, spiritual gifts.

Let me remind you of just one thing concerning each of these seven descriptive names of Holy Spirit.

(a) Comforter

When you are in pain or mourning, He is there with you as your Comforter. You may not feel the actual touch of the arms of God around you, but you can be sure they are there, because He is there. (Deuteronomy 33:27). He will ease your inner pain, fill you with God's love and sustain you with His power until you are at peace again.

(b) Counsellor

When you are confused about what to decide or do, Holy Spirit is there as your Counsellor, to impart God's wisdom to you, either directly or through someone who helps you make the right decision. (James 1:5-7). He also counsels you through the Bible that He wrote through many people.

(c) Helper

When you need a friend, a partner to get you through a tough situation or to take advantage of a great opportunity, Holy Spirit is your Helper. He can enable you to do what you cannot do on your own. He can give you favour with important people. He can arrange the release of the resources you need to succeed. (Ecclesiastes 4:9-12).

(d) Advocate

As your Advocate, Holy Spirit speaks to the Father on your behalf. He counters the devil's accusations against you, because you have been forgiven of your sins. He also works on your behalf when your reputation is attacked, both to give you peace and self-control and to work for your righteousness to be affirmed. (Psalm 103:6 NLT).

(e) Intercessor

Prayer is the most important source of power in the universe. Prayer is our God-given means of building both personal relationship and partnership with the All-Mighty. Prayer is not one-sided. We talk to God and He talks to us. As our Intercessor, Holy Spirit prays to the Father for us, just as Jesus told Peter that He had prayed for them. (Luke 22:31-32). He also inspires our praying, so that we get Divine results. I must also gladly tell you that Holy Spirit's intercession will always lead to Holy Spirit's active intervention on your behalf. Hallelujah.

Holy Spirit's intercession, either direct to God on your behalf or through you in inspired prayer, will always lead to Holy Spirit's active intervention on your behalf.

(f) Strengthener

We all have times when we feel weak. This is when we must call upon Holy Spirit to be our Strengthener. Having done so, we must act in faith as if He had answered our prayer. Joel 3:10b says: *"…. let the weak say I am strong!"* So, you must stop confessing your weakness and declare that you are strong in the Lord and in the power of His might. Then you will act as if you were strong.

By faith, you do what you think a strong person, a strong Christian, a strong believer would do in your situation. If you need to get someone else to help you be strong and act strong, then enlist their help and just do it.

(g) Standby

The key to experiencing all the things promised by the other six Holy Spirit Names is found in the final descriptive "Standby". When you get home from work or shopping or play and the television is turned off, but plugged in to the power supply, what colour is the power light? Here in Australia, it is mostly red. This signifies that the television is on standby.

What do you have to do to watch a program? Of course, you have to press the power button on your remote. What happens to the light? It turns to green. What happens to the black television screen? It comes alive with beautiful colours and simultaneously sound fills the room.

Holy Spirit as Standby is like that. He is waiting for you to switch Him into action mode. How? In chapter 2 of my book, *"You Can Prophesy – Supernatural. Simple. Safe."*, I wrote about the normal kinds of Christian activities that spark Holy Spirit into action. I mentioned:

- Prayer
- Praise and Worship
- Repentance, Righteousness and Obedience
- Faith
- Financial Giving
- Unity
- Honour
- Evangelism

Let me challenge you to stir up Holy Spirit Partnership and ministry in and through your life. He does not want to be your silent partner. He does not want to be your junior partner.

Holy Spirit does not want to be your silent partner, nor your junior partner. By faith, you must activate Him from Standby mode to active, Divine function.

God has work to do in this earth. It's up to you to surrender to Him and put your faith into action. Then, Holy Spirit will do far more good and great things for you and through you. You will be blessed, because you are being a blessing to both God and man. People will be encouraged, touched and transformed. The Lord will be glorified. How good is that! So, Go For It!

What is one thing you have learned from this teaching?

_____

What is one thing you can do to implement this teaching?

_____

Faith Declaration:

I thank You, Holy Spirit, that it is to my advantage to have You in my life. I thank You for being my Comforter Counsellor, Helper, Advocate, Intercessor, Strengthener and Standby. I switch You into active partnership mode, by my love and faith and obedience right now. I expect Your manifest Presence in me, with me, around me and through me to others this day and every day, in Jesus' mighty Name. Amen. I confess that You and I will turn every positive opportunity into a successful outcome and every negative situation into a victory for the glory of God.

4 Healing *and* Salvation

Surely our griefs (or "sickness") He Himself bore, and our sorrows (or "pains") He carried. Yet we ourselves esteemed Him stricken, Smitten of God, and afflicted. ⁵ But He was pierced through (or "wounded") for our transgressions, He was crushed for our iniquities; the chastening for our well-being (or "peace") fell upon Him, and by His scourging we are healed.

Isaiah 53:4–5 NAS

I want to share with you why I believe salvation includes physical healing. This is important, because if Jesus died for both our sickness and our sins, then by faith we can receive healing and freedom from our symptoms (because the causes thereof are healed), just as by faith we receive forgiveness and freedom from guilt, shame and condemnation.

(i) The Broad Meaning of "Salvation" includes Physical Healing

My first reason for believing that physical healing is included in the atonement suffering, sacrifice and triumph of Jesus has to do with the meaning of the word "salvation".

The very Name "Jesus" means "God saves". So, included in His Name is a statement of what Jesus came to earth to do. It wasn't just to buy believers a spiritual bus ticket to heaven or an escape pass from hell when they die.

The most prominent Hebrew word for salvation in the Old Testament is "yasa". In the New Testament the Greek words "sozo" (verb) or "soteria" (noun) are used. The way these words are used indicate that salvation is not restricted to the spiritual dimension, meaning salvation from the penalty and power of sin. Salvation also encompasses the material, circumstantial, psychological and physiological.

The Name "Jesus", which is the Greek equivalent of the Hebrew "Joshua", means "God saves" or "God is salvation". The emphasis of the New Testament is on Jesus saving lost people from sin. (Matthew 1:21–23; Luke 19:10). However, in the Gospels, Holy Spirit through the inspired writers, uses the broader meaning of salvation to specifically and explicitly include physical healing.

For example in Mark 6:56, whoever was physically sick and touched the hem of Jesus' garment, just like the woman with the issue of blood had done, was healed. The Greek word that was translated into English as "healed", in order to correctly describe what happened to the sick people, is "sozo".

This literally means that the sick were saved. They experienced a dimension of the salvation of God. The dimension they experienced was physical. They were physically saved. They were healed.

The Jews use the word "shalom", which is another multi-dimensional, whole-of-life word, as a greeting. I read once that the first Christians would greet one another, as an equivalent of the Jewish "shalom", using a derivative of "sozo", which effectively meant "how is your salvation?"

In Australia today we might ask: "How are you, my friend?" or "How're ya goin' mate?". The ancient "sozo"-based greeting, like our modern equivalent and the Jewish "shalom", was intended to ask "How is the whole of your life?"; "How is your spiritual life and your relational life and your physical life and your work life and your financial life?"

Salvation is not restricted to spiritual matters. Salvation includes physical healing and other blessings that Jesus quoted in His job description. (refer Isaiah 61:1-7; Luke 4:18-19).

On a personal level, the true and full meaning of salvation is to have wholeness of life. This occurs when you have a healthy spiritual life, which is a healthy personal relationship with our loving, holy Lord; a healthy soul (mind, will and emotions); and a healthy body. It also means having healthy relationships and healthy finances.

The Greek words translated as salvation in the New Testament, like the Hebrew word "shalom" meaning peace, are multi-dimensional, whole-of-life words. They include our spiritual life, our relational life, our physical life, our work life, our financial life and the health of our mind, will and emotions.

(ii)   The Central Salvation chapter, Isaiah 53, teaches Healing in Salvation

The first is found in Isaiah's great salvation chapter.

> *⁴Surely He (Jesus) has borne ("nasa") our griefs ("choli" sicknesses, weaknesses, and distresses) and carried ("sabal") our sorrows and pains ("makob") [...], yet we [ignorantly] considered Him stricken, smitten, and afflicted by God [...]. ⁵But He was wounded for our transgressions, He was bruised for our guilt and sins; the punishment [needed to obtain] peace and well-being for us was upon Him, and with the whip-lashes [that wounded] Him we are healed and made whole. ⁶All we like sheep have gone astray, we have turned every one to his own way; and the Lord has (put) upon Him the guilt and iniquity of us all....¹¹ My righteous servant will justify many, and He will carry ("sabal") their iniquities. ¹² ... He (Jesus) bore ("nasa") [and took away] the sin of many ...*

Isaiah 53:4–6, 11–12 AMP

• Verses 4 and 12 use the same Hebrew verb ("nasa"). This means that on the Cross, Jesus, our sinless, perfect, sacrificial substitute "bore" both our sins (v.12) and our "sicknesses" (the literal meaning of the Hebrew word "choli" in verse 4).

• Verses 4 and 11 use the same Hebrew verb ("sabal"). This tells us that Jesus "carried" both our iniquities (v.11) and "pains" (the literal meaning of the Hebrew word "makob" in verse 4).

By using this inter-related language, Holy Spirit is telling us in no uncertain terms that the very same acts of suffering, sacrifice and triumph by Jesus paid the price for both the forgiveness of our sins and the healing of our bodies.

Therefore, by faith, I can receive both forgiveness of and cleansing from my sins and healing of my sicknesses.

It is important to understand that the translators of the Hebrew words "choli" and "makob" in 15 out of 19 versions of the Bible used English words like griefs and sorrows, instead of their more literal meanings of illnesses and pains. I find it hard to understand why they would do this and difficult to not accuse the translators of unbelief.

It is easier for interpreters to say that Jesus heals our griefs and sorrows, rather than teach that He heals our bodies. It takes even less faith for people to interpret griefs and sorrows as being directly related to sin and referring to spiritual pain and sorrow, rather than meaning the healing of the very real and very painful physical and inner hurts people experience in life.

The translation of Matthew's reference to Isaiah 53:4-5, is a stinging indictment on the unbelief of the translators of the Hebrew.

When evening came, many who were demon-possessed were brought to him, and he drove out the spirits with a word and healed all the sick.[17] This was to fulfil what was spoken through the prophet Isaiah "He took up our infirmities and bore our diseases."

Matthew 8:16-17

Holy Spirit through Matthew made this clear: He wants Bible readers to understand that Jesus paid for our physical healing and deliverance from every devilish affliction, as well as for our forgiveness and freedom from the penalty and power of sin.

Jesus carried on to the Cross both our sins and our sicknesses. Therefore, we can confidently say two things.

Firstly, that God will forgive your sins, because Jesus was punished in your place. By believing in Jesus and what He did for you, you can be spiritually saved and made ready to enter God's heaven.

Secondly, that God will heal your body, because Jesus was also punished for your pains and sicknesses to be removed from you and for you to experience His Healing Power.

The teaching of Isaiah 53 is partly explained in Matthew 8:16-17. It demonstrates that Jesus was punished for both the forgiveness of our sins and the healing of our bodies.

Again I say: the Bible teaches that Christian salvation is not just spiritual; it is whole-of-life.

Of course it would be ridiculous to suggest that there is a Scripture which teaches the forgiveness of sins stopped when Jesus ascended to heaven. Similarly, there is no doctrine in the Bible that can change the nature of salvation. Healing of the physical body and deliverance from demonic afflictions are part and parcel of salvation. Therefore, for as long as there is salvation from sin, there is and must also be healing and deliverance.

All the promises of God in the Bible are received by grace through faith. Each and every Christian has to have his or her own faith to receive the spiritual salvation Jesus purchased for us all on the Cross. Similarly, every believer must also exercise the same personal faith in the Word of God and the work of Jesus in order to receive the physical salvation, the healing of our bodies, that our Lord has made available to us.

It is important for you, my reader, to grasp hold of this truth. So, again I say: Jesus paid for your full salvation. This means that, by faith in Jesus, spiritually you can be forgiven, cleansed, reconciled to God and become a friend of God. Also, by faith, you can experience peace of mind, a restored soul and physical healing.

In theological terms, we can say that physical healing is included in the atonement. Healing is included in the package of salvation that Jesus purchased for us by taking the punishment He did before and on the cross. He really was punished twice, firstly by flogging and then by crucifixion. I believe that double punishment was to clearly emphasise the fact that both forgiveness and healing are part of the salvation we receive by faith in the Word of God and in His undeserved and unearned grace.

(iii) "Shalom" is the gift of whole-of-life peace

In Isaiah 53:5b, we are told that the punishment Jesus took on our behalf brought us the shalom-peace of God.

Just a bit of Bible study will inform you that the Hebrew word "shalom" means much more than simply peace with God, which too many Christians think is all that is included in salvation.

Numbers 6:24–26 is a well-known priestly decree of God's shalom over the Israelites. It reads as an obviously whole-of-life blessing.

Psalm 38:4 uses the word shalom in direct relation to physical health – in that case it was in a negative context, meaning David's bones lacked the shalom-peace of God.

The prophecy of Jeremiah in chapter 33 verses 6–9 speaks of the shalom of God in an intertwined way with the concepts of healing, peace, cleansing, forgiveness and prosperity.

Shalom includes (a) peace with God; (b) peace within oneself; (c) peace in your body; (d) peace in your relationships and partnerships (e.g. 1 Kings 5:12); (e) peace in your finances and circumstances; and (f) peace and victory over adversity and opposition, which is the traditional meaning of peace in the context of war.

Shalom includes peace with God; peace within oneself; peace in your body; peace in your relationships and partnerships; (e) peace in your finances and circumstances; and peace and victory over adversity and opposition

---

When you realise the broad scope of the word "shalom", you can see that what Jesus purchased for us on the cross, by taking our punishment for us, was far more than only spiritual benefits. He also paid for our healing and wholeness in spirit, soul (mind, will and emotions) and body; our harmony with others; our victory in life and over the devil; and our provision for all we would need in this life to succeed in fulfilling the plan of God for and through our lives.

Why don't you stop right here and give Jesus and the Father thanks, because Jesus got what we deserved, which was punishment, so we could get what He deserved, which is whole-of-life blessing and provision.

(iv) The doctrine of salvation incorporating physical healing is revealed in both the Old and New Testaments

Bless the LORD, O my soul, And all that is within me, bless His holy name.² Bless the LORD, O my soul, And forget none of His benefits; ³ Who pardons all your iniquities, Who heals all your diseases;⁴ Who redeems your life from the pit, Who crowns you with lovingkindness and compassion; ⁵ Who satisfies your years with good things, So that your youth is renewed like the eagle.

Psalm 103:1-5

These verses of Psalm 103 teach us that with the same faith in the same Bible and the same God, we can experience forgiveness and healing and other benefits.

Malachi 4:2 talks about the Sun of Righteousness, Who has healing in His wings. This brings together in one Saviour the forgiveness of sin, the clothing with the holiness of Christ and the power of God to heal the sick.

> *14 Is any one of you sick? He should call the elders of the church to pray over him and anoint him with oil in the name of the Lord. 15 And the prayer offered in faith will make the sick person well; the Lord will raise him up. If he has sinned, he will be forgiven. 16 Therefore confess your sins to each other and pray for each other so that you may be healed. The prayer of a righteous man is powerful and effective...*
>
> *James 5:14–16*

Again we see healing and forgiveness in the very same passage of Scripture. Surely the Divine pattern and Divine promise is both clear and confirmed. The Lord your God wants you to be well, as much as He wants you to be forgiven.

Jesus demonstrated this pattern when He both forgave and healed the paralysed man, who was lowered through a roof by his four friends in order to be placed before Jesus for healing. (Mark 2:1–12). Notice that Jesus saw their faith.

It is also important to note that forgiveness may be the precursor to healing, as it was in this case.

Conclusion

Anyone who believes in Jesus and in the Word of God is equally able and qualified in Christ to receive both the forgiveness of their sins and the healing of their bodies. The sacrifice of Jesus made both forgiveness and healing available to us. We do not earn, deserve or self-qualify for these blessings. God gives them freely to us in honour of His Son, Jesus. They can only be claimed by faith.

It is important for me to emphasise that just as we cannot earn our forgiveness and our place in God's heaven, so we cannot earn our healing. The wonderful good news of the Christian Gospel is that all we need to receive God's many blessings that are freely given to us by His grace, is to have faith. We have faith in what Jesus did for each and every one of us.

No-one is more qualified or less qualified to receive healing from Jesus. He was punished so that every person of every nation and every generation could experience His full salvation for spirit, soul and body and life.

You can confidently say – and I urge you to do so out loud right now – "Healing belongs to me because of what Jesus did for me."

Many people readily accept the benefit of God's forgiveness of their sins, but fail to accept the benefit of healing for their bodies. This is partly due to the lack of preaching about healing as being included in our salvation.

Many pastors preach only part of the Gospel, the spiritual part, the "eternal life" part, which is about the forgiveness of our sins. Sadly, they ignore the natural blessings and benefits that Jesus has also made available to us – the "abundant life" aspects of salvation. The natural part of the Gospel includes healing for the mind and the body and provision for life and ministry.

For the purposes of this chapter, my key point is that whenever and wherever the "full Gospel" is preached, healing for the body is included.

I need to make my full position clear. You might ask: "Does Nick believe in doctors?" My answer is: "Yes."

I believe medical science is one aspect of the fulfilling of the prophecy in Daniel (12:4) re the "increase of knowledge". I believe the "sick need a physician" as Jesus Himself said in Mark 2:17. This is illustrated in the Old Testament by King Hezekiah's healing in Isaiah 38:21.

So, I believe in having both faith for God's Divine healing and wisdom to pursue the best medical advice and treatment that doctors can provide. However, my emphasis in this study is to say that we should go to God and His Word, not to the doctor or the pill packet, first.

I believe in having both faith for God's Divine healing and wisdom to pursue the best medical advice and treatment that doctors can provide. Doctors treat our patients, but it is God Who heals. We should go to God and His Word, not to the doctor or the pill packet, first.

The glory will always go to the Lord for our improvement and full restoration, because, as one doctor is reported to have said: We treat our patients, but it is God Who heals. This is in accord with the Bible's revelation that God gave Himself the Name "Jehovah Rapha", which means: "I am the Lord Who heals you."

The Lord has committed Himself in a covenant way to helping us get well when we are sick. Hallelujah.

Another matter I want to clarify is this: I cannot explain why some people are healed and others are not. I do not believe in blaming the patient for a lack of faith. There are many complicating and intersecting factors involved in the Divine healing of our physical conditions. I haven't got time to go into them all here.

My goal in this chapter is to inspire you to believe God for Divine healing and not be limited to medical science, nor to a "che sera sera" approach, which fatalistically represents thinking that "whatever will be, will be."

What is one thing you have learned from this teaching?

What is one thing you can do to implement this teaching?

Faith Declaration:

I thank You Lord that you have made available to me so many benefits in the Gospel and by the suffering, sacrifice and triumph of Your Divine Son Jesus, my Saviour, Healer, Provider and Lord. I praise You because I can confidently say: Healing belongs to me because of what Jesus did for me. Right now in Jesus' Name, I claim my healings and I command my body to come into line with the Word of God, and to serve the Lord and His purpose by serving me in fullness of bodily health and strength, in Jesus' Name. Amen

.

5 **Faith Confessions**
Make a Difference

⁷ So I prophesied as I was commanded. And as I was prophesying, there was a noise, a rattling sound, and the bones came together, bone to bone. ⁸ I looked, and tendons and flesh appeared on them and skin covered them, but there was no breath in them. ⁹ Then (the Lord) said to me, "Prophesy to the breath; prophesy, son of man, and say to it, 'This is what the Sovereign LORD says: Come, breath, from the four winds and breathe into these slain, that they may live.'" ¹⁰ So I prophesied as He commanded me, and breath entered them; they came to life and stood up on their feet — a vast army.

Ezekiel 37:7–10

(i)   Are you positive or negative enough to start speaking the Word of God over your life?

If you have heard the testimony of Reinhard Bonnke, you will know that his miracle ministry began because the Lord said to him: "My Words in your mouth are as powerful as My words in My mouth."

A stunning example of what the Lord said to Bonnke in action is found in the famous passage of the valley of dry bones in Ezekiel 37:1–10. As the prophet spoke what God told him to prophesy, miracle working power was released, sufficient to bring the defeated, disunited, dry, dead army to life as an effective fighting force that could liberate captives and possess inheritances wherever they went.

Twice in this passage the prophet says that he spoke the words God told him. Each time, his words of faith triggered the manifestation of the very miracles that God wanted to happen.

Understand that these bones were well and truly beyond all human repair. Only God could change their condition. They stayed defeated, dry, dead and disconnected until the prophet spoke the Word of God over them. Then they were raised up as a great and mighty army.

- How defeated, dry, dead or disconnected do you feel?

- Are you defeated, dry, dead or disconnected enough to do something about your situation?

- Are you defeated, dry, dead or disconnected enough to do something that God has ordained about your situation?

- Are you defeated, dry, dead or disconnected enough to put God's Word into action, by praising Him always and anyway, and by speaking the relevant Scriptures in His Word over your particular situation and circumstances?

The miracle in the valley of dry bones demonstrates that Divine power is released by a Christian's verbal decree of God's Word over even impossible situations and circumstances. When you speak God's Word in faith, you will activate the miracle-working power of the Holy Spirit into your situation.

(ii)   Job 22:28 explains the power of decree

Job provides another Old Testament example of this Divine principle by which words spoken in faith result in the manifestation of the things spoken. Again, I stress that Christians should speak the Word of God over their lives, families, circumstances and futures.

There is not time in this chapter to consider the powerful passage of Job 22:21–29, but I urge you to read it.

> *You shall also decide and decree a thing, and it shall be established for you; and the light [of God's favour] shall shine upon your ways.*
>
> *Job 22:28 AMP*

The Hebrew word here translated "established" literally means to "arise, stand up". In other words, what you speak over yourself and your situation will become a reality in your life.

Job 22:28 says that you shall decide and decree a thing and, by God's grace and power, it shall arise and become a reality in your life.

Job 22:28 says, in effect: you say it and God will do it. This is a key verse in understanding the power of decree.

> *You'll take delight in God, the Mighty One, and look to Him joyfully, boldly. You'll pray to Him and He'll listen; He'll help you do what you've*

promised. You'll decide what you want and it will happen; your life will be bathed in light.

Job 22:26–28 T.M.

The NIV translates the first part of verse 28 as: *"What you decide on will be done;"* The NLT version is: *"You will succeed in whatever you choose to do."*

These alternative versions emphasise the fact that God will bless what you choose to decree. Of course, the broader principle of the Word of God is that we don't speak just anything that pops into our head. We decree what God says and what God wills.

Holy Spirit through the psalmist expressed the same principle in the specific ministry of healing.

He sent His word and healed them.

Psalm 107:20

(iii)   2 Corinthians 1:20 says it best in the New Testament

Let's look at the New Testament. Here are three different versions of 2 Corinthians 1:20

For no matter how many promises God has made, they are "Yes" in Christ. And so through Him the "Amen" is spoken by us to the glory of God.

2 Corinthians 1:20 NIV

For all the promises of God find their Yes in him. That is why it is through Him that we utter our Amen to God for His glory.

2 Corinthians 1:20 ESV

For all the promises of God, whatever their number, have their confirmation in Him; and for this reason through Him also our "Amen" acknowledges their truth and promotes the glory of God through our faith.

2 Corinthians 1:20 Weymouth

Here's the key point of this verse: Jesus has said "Yes" to and made all the promises of God in the Bible available to us; but we must say the "Amen." Our words of faith are required in order for those promises to become a reality in our lives.

Jesus said "Yes" to all the promises of God, thereby making them all available to us. We must say the "Amen" in active faith, by words and actions, in order to make those promises a reality in our lives

---

(iv) The choice is yours – don't blame God

If people choose to not activate this Divine miracle-working method, to not speak in agreement with God's Word, then the promises of God will probably remain just a spiritual theory on the pages of the Bible for them.

Sadly, many uncooperative, unbelieving Christians will remain frustrated and be deceived into thinking that God does not love them or His Word does not work for them.

Let me be clear: if Christians choose to not obey, or to not speak in agreement with God's Word, then there is no guarantee that the covenant promises of God will become real in their lives simply by the Lord deciding to drop blessings and miracles into their laps, regardless of their refusal to co-operate with Him or their lack of faith in His Word. (Hebrews 3:18-4:2).

Some time ago Holy Spirit revealed this to me: when you do what the Bible says, God will do what the Bible says. Putting this revelation in the context of this chapter, it means: When by faith you say what the Bible says, God will do what the Bible says. Amen to that!

When you speak God's Words in faith, you release Holy Spirit to do good things and those good things start to happen.

(v)   Persistence pays good dividends

Warning: This is a lifestyle issue of faith, not a matter of trying it once to see if it works. I have said before that persistence overcomes enemy resistance. I need also to say, as illustrated in Jesus' parables of the unjust judge (Luke 18:1–8) and the friend who came for bread at midnight (Luke 11:5–8), you must persist in faith in order to see your miracle manifest.

God is not reluctant to bless us. Indeed He has "much more" that He wants to give us. We need to persist in order to prove the genuineness of our faith, the reality of our trust in Him and our determination to receive our miracle. Consider those who pushed through in faith to get their miracles, including the woman with the issue of blood (Luke 8:43–48), the Syrophonecian mother (Matthew 15:21–28) and the four friends who broke a hole in someone's roof in order to get a miracle from Jesus for their paralysed buddy. (Mark 2:1–12).

Persisting in faith pays miraculous dividends

Christians must know what the Bible says, believe what the Bible says and say what the Bible says!

By faith, let the weak, say "I am strong." (Joel 3:10).

By faith, let the intimidated Gideon, say: "I am a mighty man of valour." (Judges 6:12).

By faith, let the childless Abraham, say: "I am a father of many nations." (Genesis 17:5).

By faith, let those who fear they cannot, say: "I can do all things through Christ Who strengthens me." (Philippians 4:13). Note: Don't say "I can't", when God says "you can".

Another reason for persisting in faith with the confession of God's word is found in Romans 10:17. As you speak the Word of God, your own faith will grow, so that you can believe for the manifestation of the promises of God. As your faith grows, you will not let the devil, or people or life's circumstances, life's seasons or life's disappointments rob you of your blessings or miracles.

You will start to believe again that:

- your life will be better
- your marriage will improve,
- your children will return to the Lord
- your finances will increase and your debts decrease,
- your body will be healed,
- your mind will be at peace,

- your emotions will experience the joy of the Lord,

- your mourning will be turned to dancing,

- your spiritual enemies will retreat

- the defeat they were trying to impose upon you will become a victory for the glory of the Lord

- your ministry will be abundantly blessed.

Of course the devil will fight you all the way to rob you of your inheritance in every area of life. Praise God, there is a way to defeat him and be blessed despite his impeding efforts.

They triumphed over him (the devil) by Blood of the Lamb and by the word of their testimony;

Revelation 12:11

These believers spoke the words of the Bible and their own stories of God's partnership in and favour over their lives. When they did this, the devil retreated from them, just as he did when Jesus resisted him with the word of God, when He was tempted in the wilderness. (Luke 4:1-13).

Why do spoken words help defeat the devil? Because God has ordained it to be so.

Remember the words have to be spoken in faith, and be in agreement with God's Word.

What is one thing you have learned from this teaching?

What is one thing you can do to implement this teaching?

Faith Declarations:

•   In Christ, I have been delegated Divine authority (Luke 10:19; Matthew 28:18-20). In Jesus' Name, I speak Divine protection and provision into being over myself, my family and my church family, each and all. (Psalms 91 and 121; John 10:10).

•   I will not fear what man or life or the devil do to me, because The Lord is on my side and no weapon formed against me shall prosper. (Psalm 118:6-7; Isaiah 54:17)

•   In Jesus' name, I speak God's Peace over my life and family. I declare Peace in my mind; in my emotions; in my body; in my family and in all my relationships and partnerships. (Isaiah 53:4,5)

•   I thank You Father God that Your mercies are new every morning. (Lamentations 3:21-25). I thank You Lord that today I will not be dominated by any of the negatives of my distant or recent past. In Jesus' Name, I receive Your forgiveness and give it to people who have hurt or offended me. I also receive my healing and freedom from every such thing. I bless my new day and my future in Jesus' Name with the blessings of Heaven above and of the earth, because I have All-Mighty God as my Divine Helper. (Ephesians 1:3; Genesis 49:22,25,26).

6

Journey to
Double Portion
Gilgal

When the Lord was about to take Elijah up to heaven in a whirlwind, Elijah and Elisha were on their way from Gilgal.² Elijah said to Elisha, "Stay here; the Lord has sent me to Bethel." But Elisha said, "As surely as the Lord lives and as you live, I will not leave you"

⁹ When they had crossed, Elijah said to Elisha, "Tell me, what can I do for you before I am taken from you?" "Let me inherit a double portion of your spirit," Elisha replied.

2 Kings 2:1–2 and 9

The journey Elisha took to inherit the double portion has much to tell us today about how we can position ourselves to receive a double portion anointing from God. In Elisha's case it was for ministry. For us, it may be for ministry or business or family or any area of our life. The Lord wants to equip and resource His people to succeed in all seven significant areas of society, namely: family, church, government, education, business, media and art/sport/entertainment.

There were four places the two prophets visited on this journey. Of course, the refusal of Elisha to stop at any of those places as Elijah instructed him to is a lesson in itself. It's not about disobeying our overseers, because both prophets knew the instruction was not for obedience but to test Elisha's persistence in pursuing Elijah's mantle.

We will not reach our full potential in God without persistence that is fuelled by a hunger for more of Him and more from Him.

The four places Elijah and Elisha visited have some great lessons for us, regarding how to position ourselves for greater things in God. Let's look at what happened when Israel came to Gilgal.

(i)   Circumcision

Gilgal was the place where every man in Israel was circumcised and where they celebrated the Passover for the first time in a generation. These two things are symbolic of being born again. Of course, no one can be anointed, much less receive a double portion, without first becoming a born again child of God, through repentance and faith in Jesus Christ.

But let me mention some things that are more subtle and yet very significant about the circumcision at Gilgal:

Romans 2:25–29 tells us that the primary symbolism of physical circumcision is to represent the circumcision of the heart. This means a cutting away of the old, worldly way of life fuelled by the sin-loving Adamic nature. Instead, we live in a Christ-like way, empowered by Holy Spirit, demonstrating holiness of life in thoughts, words and actions.

Let me ask you to think about this question: Why did God choose that sign of the Covenant?

Why did the Lord not choose a tattoo, whether hidden or public? Leviticus 19:28 rules out that option.

Why not the famous American Indian wrist-scarring? That is ruled out by the fact that the only human blood God ordained to be shed was that of His Own Son, our Lord Jesus Christ, who suffered, sacrificed His life and rose triumphantly again for our salvation.

What about the love-slave symbol of ear-piercing? (Exodus 21:2-6). Paul calls himself the New Testament equivalent of this in Romans 1 verse 1. The Lord in His infinite wisdom chose a covenant sign that was far richer in meaning than this.

Now I am not going to describe male circumcision here, but I will explain the symbolism I believe underlies God's choice of this particular covenant sign.

(a) Circumcision indicates how very personal our relationship with God is and that there is nothing in our lives which is too private for God. Let's face it, God is omniscient. (Hebrews 4:13). There is nothing that is hid from His sight anyway, so why bother trying, the way Adam and Eve did? It didn't work for them. It won't work for us.

(b) Circumcision represents giving our sexuality to God. This means that Christ-followers choose to live sexually according to the boundaries in the Word of God, which exclude sex outside of marriage and homosexuality.

(c) Circumcision signifies that our productivity and creativity depend on God.

Circumcision represents (a) not trying to hide anything from our all-seeing, all-knowing God; (b) living in sexual purity and obedience to God's Word; (c) trusting God for and partnering with Him in areas of the creativity and productivity of our lives and ministries.

(ii)   Protection in times of vulnerability

Gilgal also testifies that God will protect us in our times of vulnerability. Perhaps you know how distracting an unattended splinter in your finger can be. Imagine what a couple of stones in your shoes would feel like. Now multiply those by a hundred or a thousand and you might have an idea of how the Jewish army was feeling after their un-anaesthetised circumcisions. Those soldiers were incapable of fighting or resisting their enemy. If the Jericho under-12 girls arm-wrestling team had come out against them, the girls would have won easily.

The Lord protected them in their time of vulnerability. He has promised to do the same for you and me.

> *Even when I walk through the darkest valley, I will not be afraid, for you are close beside me. Your rod and your staff protect and comfort me.*
>
> *Psalm 23:4 NLT*

When I have been stretched to my limit physically, emotionally or spiritually, I have asked the Lord to keep any further attacks or pressure from the enemy from me until I was replenished. You can do that too. God will protect, sustain, heal and re-energise you.

> *No temptation has overtaken you except what is common to mankind. And God is faithful; He will not let you be tempted beyond what you can bear. But when you are tempted, He will also provide a way out so that you can endure it.*
>
> *1 Corinthians 10:13*

(iii)   Inner healing and renewing the mind

Gilgal literally means "rolling". The site was named this because of what the Lord said.

> *Today I have rolled away the reproach of Egypt from you.*
>
> *Joshua 5:9*

In other words, as they submitted to physical circumcision, God did some internal miracles for them. Their circumcision at Gilgal also represents the healing of their souls and the renewing of their minds.

The Lord removed the stigma of their slavery in Egypt from them. The Hebrew word translated "reproach" in that verse is "cherpah", which also means "shame; disgrace; contempt; scorn".

Firstly, God removed from them and healed them of their feelings of inferiority and shame. They had a 400-year history, which is at least five generations of poverty and slavery and abuse.

What mind-set would you have about yourself if you were in the position where you could say: "I am a sanitary worker, my dad was a sanitary worker, his dad was a sanitary worker, and so on?" With apologies to those in this field of work, can you imagine what it must do to a person's thinking about their potential and future if their family history, perhaps going back to their great-great-grandfather and beyond even that, was the same lowly position?

Praise God, you can break out of that and break into your true Divine potential and destiny. The founders of the movement I have served my whole Christian life, the Apostolic Church of Australia, which was birthed by pioneers from the Apostolic Churches of

Wales, Scotland and England, did. Those founding leaders were Welsh miners, whose fathers were Welsh miners, whose fathers were Welsh miners etc. They rose up under the calling and anointing of the Lord to be mighty apostolic, miracle-working church planters and builders whose influence has circled the globe. They were led by the Spirit with supernatural prophetic revelation. They had passion for God, for His Word and for people everywhere. The miracle-working power of the Lord was evident in their ministries. In Australia they filled every town hall in every capital city. This was unprecedented. Some of the miracles God did were literally front page news.

God had to break similar, but worse, negative mind-sets off Israel before they could step into their new and true destiny.

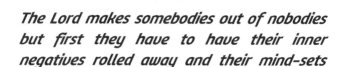

The Lord makes somebodies out of nobodies but first they have to have their inner negatives rolled away and their mind-sets changed.

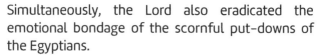

Simultaneously, the Lord also eradicated the emotional bondage of the scornful put-downs of the Egyptians.

You too must, with the Lord's help, step away from and step out of the grip of your negative past, including both bad experiences and bad words spoken over you, and step into the mercies, blessings and power of God that are new every morning.

Don't let your past rob you of your future destiny. No one can experience a double portion if they think they are a good-for-nothing, poor, inferior person, or if they are paralysed by fear, as the Jewish army was when Goliath taunted them. Through the words of the Bible, God says we are His chosen sons and daughters, His powerful people, His ambassadors, who represent and re-present Christ on earth.

No one can experience a double portion if they think they are a good-for-nothing, poor, inferior person, or if they are paralysed by fear

(iv)   Promised Land benefits and battles

There is another significant thing that happened at Gilgal. The daily manna stopped; but the Bible says "*that year they ate the produce of Canaan*". (Joshua 5:12).

Like Israel, you must choose one of three alternative lifestyles, namely, (a) slavery in Egypt, which represents people who are not yet saved and are still slaves to sin; (b) a Christian life of wandering in the wilderness; or (c) taking your promised land, your inheritance in Christ and fulfilling your divine potential and God-given purpose in life. Each option has a price tag and a set of consequences.

(a) Slaves are in bondage and have a victim mentality. If they are lucky, they have a roof over their head and enough food and water to survive. But their workload is far more than it should be and they may often be punished, even if they don't deserve it, and possibly far more severely than their mistake warranted. No-one would want to be a slave and certainly not the devil's slave, because he is the hardest and worst slave-master of them all.

Sadly, some people in the world today can't get out of literal slavery. Others are in terrible circumstances of life and they cannot see a way out, emotionally, financially or physically. They are too scared to ask for help. They feel they have nowhere else to go. We Christians need to pray for such people and help the ones we can.

(b) Wilderness people simply survive and go nowhere with their life. They are glad to be free, but stuck in a lifestyle of just getting by spiritually and in other ways. Their faith is not well developed enough to reap the benefits of the new covenant Jesus initiated and fulfilled all the conditions for on the Cross.

Their life is just a cycle of going round and round the same mulberry bush or up and down the same mountain, year after year, like people who grow old without ever growing up. They have no real purpose, vision, dream or goals that motivate them to get up every morning. They do not have the personal relationship with God that puts them in the centre of His will for their lives. They do not have the personal partnership with the Lord that empowers them to maximize who they are and what their impact is on their world and generation. They exemplify mediocrity of Christian thinking and living.

(c) Promised Land Christians do not have the best of everything just drop into their lap. They must fight the good fight of faith for their prosperity and freedom. For Israel, as they came into Canaan, the manna stopped and the fighting began in earnest.

Jesus Himself said we will not enter into the abundant life He came to give us without having to confront the devil for it. Jesus said the devil would do everything in his power to stop us inheriting the best that God has for us. (John 10:10).

Promised Land Christians are committed to advancing the Kingdom of God on earth, in all seven spheres of society, namely, Family, Church, Government, Education, Business, Media and Art-Sport-Entertainment.

If you want to be a Promised Land Christian, you will need to use your faith and every spiritual weapon the Lord has made available to you.

You cannot be a double portion Christian if you think God is just going to drop more blessings and resources into your lap. You have to go out and use what you already have to possess your promised land. When you use what you have, God will give you more. That's the principle of sowing and reaping. God will always give you a harvest greater than what you sow.

(v)   Now is the time to start or start again

.... And who knows but that you have come to your royal position for such a time as this?"

Esther 4:14

For He says, "In the time of My favour I heard you, and in the day of salvation I helped you." I tell you, now is the time of God's favour, now is the day of salvation.

2 Corinthians 6:2

There is another lesson of note that we can learn from Gilgal. They had not observed Circumcision or Passover for almost 40 years.

It doesn't matter if you have neglected God or been disobedient to Him in the past, what counts is what you do now, this year and for the rest of your life. Get on board with God and His purpose for your life, either for the first time or again, starting right now.

God is faithful and merciful. He knows how we are formed, He remembers that we are dust. (Psalm 103:14). He is the God of the second chance and the twenty second chance and the two thousand and second chance. But be aware even God's patience does have limits, so don't put Him to the test.

You need to get your spiritual act together. You need to get your relationship and partnership with God in correct order and function. Holy Spirit will help you do these things. When you do this consistently, you will become a promised land Christian. Then, in the words of Isaiah (1:19 and 55:2), you will enjoy what is good and delight in the richest of both heavenly and earthly blessings and provisions from the Lord.

What is one thing you have learned from this teaching?

_____

What is one thing you can do to implement this teaching?

_____

Faith Declaration:

I thank You Lord for giving me new life within and without. I am so grateful that You have rolled away all the negativity of my past life. I am grateful for Your Holy Spirit helping me live pleasing unto You and in close relationship and partnership with You. I praise You for calling me and empowering me to think and live and act like a promised land Christian. I thank You for every victory in my life, past, present and future. Lord I dedicate myself completely, in a fresh way, to You today. I commit myself to walking with You and for You by faith. I look forward to receiving my full inheritance in Christ here on earth and in Heaven for all eternity and I declare it will be so, in Jesus' Mighty Name. Amen

.
_____

7

Journey to
Double Portion

Bethel, Jericho and Jordan

² Elijah said to Elisha, "Stay here; the LORD has sent me to Bethel." But Elisha said, "As surely as the LORD lives and as you live, I will not leave you." So they went down to Bethel. ...⁹ When they had crossed, Elijah said to Elisha, "Tell me, what can I do for you before I am taken from you?" "Let me inherit a double portion of your spirit," Elisha replied.

2 Kings 2:2 and 9

In this chapter, we continue to walk with the two prophets Elijah and Elisha on the way to receiving our double portion using the same spiritual principles as Elisha did.

They started at Gilgal and went to three other places, which also have spiritual significance and lessons for us.

(i)   Bethel, the House of God

The second place the two prophets went to on this double portion journey was Bethel, which literally means "the House of God". This was the place where Jacob dreamed of angels ascending and descending on God's Stairway to Heaven. In his prophetic dream, Jacob saw the Lord, Who made a covenant of protection and prosperity with him. (Genesis 28:12–15).

(a)   Bethel teaches us about our response to the Presence and Partnership of God

This Divine encounter and Divine promise gave Jacob real confidence about his future, so much so that he immediately committed himself to a lifestyle of financial tithing. It's important to note that this giving was voluntary on Jacob's part. It was a gift of gratitude, not fulfilling a law. Jacob willingly, cheerfully and heartfully chose to give to God a tenth of his income and increase, as a lifestyle.

(Genesis 28:21). This is how the apostle Paul was told by Holy Spirit to describe godly giving in 2 Corinthians 9:8.

Financial giving to God is a heart matter. I wrote about this in my first book "*You Can Prophesy – Supernatural. Simple. Safe.*"

In Malachi 3:7 The Lord says His people have strayed from relationship with Him. The result is that He has withdrawn His Presence from them. The absence of the Presence of God has resulted in them being under a curse and suffering losses from various crop-destroying pests and diseases. They were in a very similar position to that described in Haggai 1:5,6,9–11 and 2:15–19.

In this passage in Malachi the Lord indicates that he misses and covets their company. He wants to be with His people. So, He tells them how this can happen.

Of course, we all know how to get closer to the Lord. We can read our Bible more. We can pray, praise and worship more. We can go to church and connect groups more. Maybe we can serve and witness more. We can examine our heart and lifestyle to see if we have any sin problems.

God says in verse 7 that obedience or disobedience in regard to tithing is a relationship issue.

Now, consider what Jesus taught in John 14:21 and 23. Those who love God, obey Him ... and they are rewarded with His presence. So a Christian's disobedience is a love issue, a relationship issue.

That's why the Lord says in Malachi, if you want to return to Me in relationship, then show Me you love Me by obeying My principle of tithing.

I have a number of favourite sayings. The following one is so good that it deserves to be in the Bible. I believe it encapsulates what God is saying in these verses.

"You can give without loving" (say, by paying your taxes, electricity bills and credit card debts); "but you cannot love without giving."

Here's the principle that is revealed in this passage from Malachi 3: If you have a problem with giving to God, then you have a problem with loving God.

Financial giving to God is a relationship issue. If you have a problem with giving to God, then you have a problem with loving God. You can give without loving, but you cannot love without giving.

If you are a son of God, you will have real confidence about your future and you will be unafraid to live by faith. This is because you know God, His Nature and His Word. He is a rewarder of those who love Him, believe in Him and obey Him. (Hebrews 11:6).

In the area of your finances, and in every other area of life, you can't expect God's reward, nor His double portion, if you haven't got the faith to live your life financially God's way.

If we want to receive the double portion, we've got to believe for it and then put our faith into action ... as a lifestyle.

(b)   Bethel reminds us that God is faithful to His promises and will do far, far more for us His children, than we could ever ask or think. (Matthew 7:11; Ephesians 3:20).

(c)   Bethel also represents a desire to know God, a hunger to be in His presence and a commitment to the house of God.

It's not good enough to want God's blessing or power, we must want Him. Don't seek only the gift, seek the Giver. Don't seek only the healing, seek the Healer.

One thing have I desired of the LORD,
that will I seek after – that I may dwell in
the house of the LORD all the days of my

life, to behold the beauty of the LORD, and to enquire in His temple.

Psalm 27:4

We can ask God for many things, all the promises of God in fact, but what really matters to the Lord is, do we want God Himself? Or, do we only want what God can do for us?

Do we love God with all our heart and soul and mind and strength? Or, do we just love His blessing?

(d)   Bethel, the House of God, reminds us of the importance of being active and consistent members of your local church.

I want you to notice that twice in this verse (Psalm 27:4) the togetherness aspect of Christianity is emphasised. The Psalmist mentions the house and the temple of the Lord, the place of the gathering together of the people of God.

So let me ask you this question: How much of a priority is church in your life? Can people see that you seek first the Kingdom of God, because you are a regular church-goer?

Let us consider and give attentive, continuous care to watching over one another, studying how we may stir up (stimulate and incite) to love and helpful deeds and noble activities, [25] not forsaking or neglecting to assemble together [as believers], as is the habit of some people, but admonishing (warning, urging, and encouraging) one another, and all the more faithfully as you see the day (of our Lord's return) approaching.

Hebrews 10:25 AMP.

We often hear how bad habits can be very depleting in our lives. We also need to recognise that some habits, traditions and customs are good for us.

Bad habits can be very depleting in our lives. Some habits and traditions such as church participation, which was the custom of both Jesus and Paul, are actually very good for us.

Be like Jesus (Luke 4:16) and Paul (Acts 17:2) whose custom it was to go to church. Don't be like Doubting Thomas who was missing when Jesus turned up; nor like the 380 who missed the visitation of Holy Spirit in the Upper Room. Remember that in 1 Corinthians 15:6, Jesus appeared to more than five hundred at one time.

If the things of God such as prayer, reading God's Word, financial giving, personal and church worship and serving the Lord in church and in the world are not your custom, how can you expect to enter into the double portion?

All things are given to us by the Grace of God (that's His part); but we receive them by active faith (that's our part).

What I have said so far in regard to the double portion journey, is that it starts with salvation (Gilgal) and continues with discipleship in the local church (Bethel). The church and the relationships we build and learn from are fundamental to building strong faith in the Lord and His Word. This helps us mature as Christians and to learn how to walk by faith in all areas of life. (2 Corinthians 5:7).

(ii)   Jericho,   the   place   of   overcoming adversity and opposition

The third place prophets Elijah and Elisha visited was Jericho, where Joshua and his army saw God flatten the city's walls as they obeyed His strategy for victory.

If we want the double portion, we've got to do things God's Way and we've got to walk by faith. For

Joshua and his army, that included taking control of their own tongues. They marched around the city in silence. That way no negative talk about the battle was possible. In World War 2 there was a saying to warn people about the power of their tongues: "Loose lips sink ships."

Israel faced the enemy together, not alone, believing for the supernatural partnership of the Holy Spirit. When the battle was to be joined, they shouted confidently and fought like victors, not victims.

We've got to face our enemies, within and without, and believe God for the victory. As Christ's Church, we are to be the devil's nightmare, as we enforce the victory Jesus has won over the devil and all his works. Jesus is our Commander-in-Chief, which is how He revealed Himself to Joshua prior to the battle.

Let me also remind you of the principle found in James 4:7. You cannot defeat the enemy unless and until you are submitted to God.

(iii)   Jordan, where miracles happen

The double portion journey starts with salvation, continues with discipleship in the local church, progresses by overcoming adversity and opposition and fourthly, it requires the believer to step into a lifestyle of faith that enables them to experience the favour of God and supernatural partnership of the Lord.

It is common for Spirit-filled preachers like myself to see the symbolism of Israel crossing the River Jordan into their Promised Land as representing receiving the baptism in the Holy Spirit, because crossing the Red Sea is interpreted as the type of becoming born again.

(a)   Through the example of Jesus, we learn the Jordan represents the place of experiencing an Open Heaven, the Father's Voice and the Power of Holy Spirit.

The River Jordan is where the ministry of Jesus started. Mark 1:9 tells us that Jesus was baptised both in water and in Holy Spirit and heard the affirming Voice of the Father at the River Jordan.

So, the River represents a place of an open Heaven. It speaks of Holy Spirit empowerment to do the work of the ministry that we have been called to do. The River Jordan is the launching place for every Christian to live a supernatural lifestyle. (Acts 1:8). It is the place where God opens our eyes and ears to the invisible world of Holy Spirit and the angels, as Jesus promised Nathaniel. (John 1:51).

Water baptism is symbolic of dying to the old worldly life and Holy Spirit baptism is representative of living in the new supernatural life of the Spirit.

Sadly, many Christians today only know one baptism, not the two baptisms Jesus set as an example for us to follow. Jesus wants every Christian to be a supernatural son and servant of God. This is why He sent Holy Spirit on the day of Pentecost to give the church "power", Divine power. (Acts 1:8).

(b)   No turning back, at this final stage, from the Promised Land lifestyle of faith and supernatural Holy Spirit Partnership.

Both baptisms represent an attitude of no turning back, as did the crossing over of Joshua and the Jews.

The River Jordan also represents the final stage in the journey from the wilderness, the time of preparation, to the edge of the Promised Land and into the land of fulfilment.

According to 2 Kings 6:2 the River Jordan was the place where Elisha's faith and double portion anointing and spiritual authority was used to miraculously raise a borrowed axe head that had fallen into the murky river.

Just as the prophet threw in a stick, so you have to sow before you reap; you have to step out in faith; you have to do something in order to step into the supernatural and keep on doing it so that it becomes a lifestyle of Divine relationship and partnership between you and God.

Elisha inherited the double portion because he had the faith to pursue, to see and to do. It's interesting to note that when you compare the number of miracles associated with Elijah and Elisha in the Bible, you find that Elisha is credited with twice as many miracles as his mentor, Elijah. How often it is that the generation who stand on the shoulders of others achieves more than they did. The ceiling of the previous generation becomes the floor of their successors.

By contrast to Elisha, Esau didn't value God's promises, so he sold his double portion inheritance of the first-born son to his brother Jacob. He wanted food now. How many have missed out on their double portion, because they hunger for the immediate satisfaction of the things of this world?

Elisha also demonstrated holy boldness as he stepped out in faith after fulfilling the condition Elijah had specified would qualify him to receive the double portion.

He struck the water as he had seen Elijah do and boldly called out "where is the Lord God of Elijah?"

In other words, he said to God: "I've done my bit, so Lord now it's Your turn; the ball is in Your court." In New Testament terms we would say: "Lord, I expect Divine action now, based on a covenant fulfilled by Jesus and on my obedience to the promises and principles of Your Word."

Where is the Lord God of Elijah? I've done my bit, so Lord now it's Your turn; the ball is in Your court. Lord, I expect Divine action now, based on a covenant fulfilled by Jesus and on my obedience to the promises and principles of Your Word.

When you are not sure what to do to receive your miracle, do what you have been taught to do or what you have seen your mentors do. Every time, when you do what the Bible says, you can be sure God will do what the Bible says.

Elisha's first miracle of the parting of the River Jordan, teaches us this: there really are no "suddenlys" and certainly none that "just happen".

Jesus lived 30 years of preparation and learning the Word and being obedient. Then came the Voice and the Spirit. Most of the people in the upper room on the day of Pentecost had for three years given up everything to follow Jesus. Then, in obedience to Him, they spent 10 days and nights in the upper room, worshipping, praying, praising, waiting on the Lord, encouraging one another in the Scriptures. After that, the Spirit came in mighty power.

(iv)   What is your lifestyle?

Are you in some kind of slavery or bondage situation within yourself or in life's circumstances? The Lord can set you free.

Are you wandering round and round in a spiritual wilderness, just staying alive, bored in your faith, doing nothing to fulfil God's covenant purposes and not receiving all His covenant blessings and resources?

Or are you a Promised Land Christian, who is not fazed by adversity or opposition? Are you getting on with what God has called you to do, whether you can see great fruit or not? If you are, take courage, because Galatians 6:9 tells you that if you do not grow weary in well doing, you will reap a harvest.

God has called you to be more than a conqueror. (Romans 8:37). That means you not only win for yourself but for others; and you do not conquer for yourself, but to set captives free so they can also be victorious, prosper and help others.

You double portion blessings, resources and miracles are on their way. Your victories are guaranteed by the victory of Jesus. You are a walking power-house for God, because Holy Spirit lives in you. You can make a difference in your world and in the lives of people around you, because as you step out in faith, Holy Spirit steps out with you.

What is one thing you have learned from this teaching?

_____

What is one thing you can do to implement this teaching?

_____

Faith Declaration:

I thank You Lord for enabling me to grow from faith to faith, strength to strength, glory to glory, victory to victory and anointing to anointing. By faith I step into my next level place in God. I believe for and speak into being the double portion plus of Heaven to be manifest in every area of my life, family and ministry in Jesus' Name. Lord I dedicate myself afresh to a life of true and full discipleship of following Jesus, according to Your Word and the leading of Your Spirit. I believe Your Senior and Supernatural Partnership will be in increasing evidence in my life, for the glory of my King, Jesus, in Whose Name I make this declaration. Amen.

ABOUT THE AUTHOR

 Nick Watson has been happily married to Lynne since 1970. They have 3 children, Kylie, Simon and Rebekah; 4 (so far) grandchildren Katie, Rennick, Craig and Aiden; and 1 great-granddaughter, Riley.

Nick is the Founder, Principal Prophet, Author and Teacher, and People Builder of Prophetic Power Ministries.

He was for years the Senior Pastor of Bayside Christian Family (Apostolic) Church, a thriving Spirit-filled church in Brisbane, Queensland. Australia.

Nick has been a recognised prophet in the Apostolic Church Australia for more than 25 years. He has served in various denominational leadership roles.

Nick has preached and prophesied throughout Australia and overseas, with a signs-following ministry.

YOUR FEEDBACK

If this book "Holy Spirit Faith Food Snack Pack" has encouraged your faith, please share your testimony with us at the email address below.

CONTACT Nick Watson

If you desire to contact Nick concerning a ministry engagement at your church, group, camp or leaders event please visit our website:

www.youcanprophesy.com

 www.facebook.com/nickjwatson.ycp

 email: youcanprophesy@gmail.com

OTHER BOOKS by Nick Watson

Faith Food Snack Pack – Overcoming

Faith Food Snack Pack – Good News

Faith Food Snack Pack – Healthy Soul

Lessons From My Dog – 33 Faith Lifters

You Can Prophesy – Supernatural. Simple. Safe.